Aurélienne Dauguet

COMMUNICATION BEYOND THE VEIL

From being a sceptic to my aura-medium-center

MERANO-VERLAG

Content

Theoretical and practical trainings of the AURA-MEDIUM-CENTER:

1. CHANNELING MEDIUM TRAINING: OVERVIEW OF THE CURRICULUM

2. AURA THERAPY TRAINING: OVERVIEW OF A 6 W/E CURRICULUM

INTRODUCTION

Behind this partial biographical account lies a powerful message for you. It is a reminder that you also possess the capacities to relate to the various dimensions within yourself (to the deeper layers of your unconscious, to your body and its functions) as well as to the various levels of consciousness in the universe.

Communication is the basis of existence: everything is in a lively exchange, similar to the natural rhythm of inhaling and exhaling, which keeps everything alive.

Everything in the universe is connected to each other and constantly interacting with each other. This applies to incarnated beings in the material world as well as those in the spiritual dimensions and also to the interaction between the physical and spiritual planes.

Since human beings are spiritual beings, they have the ability to receive and send information from this world to the afterlife and back. We are able to get impulses from our body and parts of our personality. We have the latent ability to connect verbally, telepathically, and through the senses with our Higher Self, as well as with non-incarnated entities.

We humans have forgotten that we can exchange thoughts with the universe at any time, as well as receive very individual answers. Or has this ability of universal communication been stolen from us?

I, too, have partially repressed my talents. Until I was shown that units of consciousness accompany and support us and that we can communicate with, as well as with the deceased and other disembodied beings.

Through their empathetic messages, they led me to found the Aura-Medium-Center. Its meaning and purpose as well as the

content of the training is explained in detail at the end of the
book.

PART 1: "WE DON´T BELIEVE IN ANYTHING"

As far back as I can remember, I carry another dimension within me along with my own "unity of consciousness". It communicates in the form of voices, inner images, feelings and occasionally also as unequivocal knowledge. In addition, I receive impulses from these higher levels, as if I was being physically pushed and stimulated to perform certain actions. In everyday life, I receive clear cues that highlight and illuminate important information and are accompanied by a certain excitement. It's as if this dimension is emphasizing chosen pieces of knowledge for me to inevitably draw my attention to them. This can be audible, visual or olfactory. Early in my youth, an acquaintance claimed that my "over-self" was very developed. It's an interesting explanatory model. However, today I offer a deeper exploration of the subject.
When I am alone, I am always perceiving a presence around me. So I am never feeling alone. On the contrary, I repeatedly experience the need to withdraw in order to devote myself to my inner companionship. I welcome solitude and enjoy the freedom and stillness in which my internalized encounters take place.

Even before the age of 2, as soon as I was able to move independently, I enjoyed sitting under the big table with the long tablecloth. It reached almost down to the floor and provided me with a wonderful protection.
While remaining in this obscure comfort, I would sink into a state of meditation. Not only did I feel a deep peace, but I experienced states of infinity, freedom, bliss, the fulfillment of beingness, which expressed themselves in an extremely beneficial spiritual fulfilment and a sensual enjoyment. Everything felt more subtle and real there than in the outside

world. There, under the long tablecloth, I experienced the eternal presence of my being. There I withdrew into "my world" to find myself again and become one with everything that is. My gaze was able to grasp further and deeper than in everyday life: My perception expanded into infinity and at the same time I could see behind and through things. I communicated with everything through telepathy or, even better, I understood many things through my spontaneous clairvoyance. I just knew and got answers in the form of sensations, both through the senses and internal. Only in my inner world could I really relax and trust. Only there did I feel a real togetherness. That was the only place I felt at home. There, under the tablecloth, I saw or perhaps created phases of my later life. Occasionally, I experience situations in my life that feel very much like "déjà-vu". Without a doubt, I experience them in reality, exactly as they were played to me mentally.

There was no constraint from outside, no intrusion into my imagination, no noise. Everything there was pure, quiet and comprehensible to me.

As time went by, my "escapes" under the table were repeatedly interrupted by my mother, making it difficult for me to settle down. She couldn't understand my need to retreat. In fact, she was extremely concerned that something was wrong with me. It is not normal for a child to withdraw quietly and into the dark. A child should play and run around. And so, I had to come out of hiding and my mother would send me into the garden. She meant I should move and get busy. I internalized this belief, and it shaped me into adulthood, during which I exhibited a kind of overactivity. I was driven and felt like I was never accomplishing anything and that nothing was ever happening in my life.

My family had no understanding of my character. They felt unsettled, if not frightened, by my existence. My mother punished me. My father laughed at me. I am special, peculiar, different.

Although the members of my family considered themselves non-compliant, I was a challenge to them. Their leitmotif was "We believe in nothing, only in what we see". This means, among other things, "We do not believe in God."

For my part, I also believed in what I saw. But I could perceive other dimensions than what my family did.

The great advantage of my atheistic upbringing is that I have acquired the habit of checking and questioning many things for myself. In addition, my cartesian upbringing encouraged me to think things over logically and coherently. I am very grateful for that. I was never gullible, not even during my time in the New Age movement. I made a pact with my inner guidance. Should my path in life or in my thought construct be false, out of touch with reality or distorted, I should receive warning signs. And life does send me wake up calls. They make me aware of my self-deception like through a magnifying glass.

Before I make an important decision, I focus on having it confirmed by my higher instance. At one time, I asked my guides to provide me with the name of my first shop in Augsburg. For me, their answer would also symbolize the approval of my higher self. It meant that my project was blessed by and in alignment with my soul. I waited in vain for days, weeks, and even several months. Those around me became impatient and my tax adviser threatened me with high taxes if I didn't invest the money in time.

Finally, I was able to let go and at some point, while I was busy with something completely different the name Lumina unexpectedly came to mind. I researched its etymology. And yes, that was the correct term meaning the light, for my spiritual shop that provided items to raise the vibration.

My distinctness and my unrecognized skills

A disturbing realization of my childhood was the discovery that the people around me had different perceptions than mine. This imparted to me the feeling that I was an outsider, that I was different, and ultimately that something was wrong with me.

My distinctness had a provocative or awakening role. I have always addressed topics and situations that were repressed, controversial or still unknown, such as: death, extraterrestrials, wanting to learn German (when everyone still hated Germans), wanting to learn Russian (when everyone was afraid of the communists), chemtrails, chakras (although the Zurich librarian claimed that chakra is a French word), living abroad, etc. That hasn't changed to this day: I keep coming up with topics that trigger my family.

Over the years, the feeling of being misunderstood has been transformed by an unshakable trust in my inner voice and, above all, the courage to follow it.
I have learned to adapt and still do exactly what is essential to me.
I have learned to wander between my outer life and my inner perceptions. Over time, I managed to build a bridge. For years, spirituality has given impetus to all areas of my life.

Childhood, depression, and doubt

After realizing that my clairvoyance was interfering with my family and that I was being punished for it, I decided to go "normal" and stop mentioning my perceptions. I became very taciturn, withdrawn and depressed. Finally, it got quiet around me. No one noticed that I had lost all zest for life. In fact, I managed to partially suppress my abilities. The price was a depressed childhood.

Even the music of the spheres, which I could hear during my childhood, became silent forever. To this day I am haunted by nostalgia for these unworldly sounds (not from this world).

During this phase of my life, I developed compassion and empathy. Out of the pain, I developed a sense of security and integrity and found harmony with my true self. Thus, I am able to encourage and strengthen my fellow humans to seek and find their path.

As a child, I was fascinated by death. Once, I asked my mother: "What happens when you die?" She replied: "Then it's all over and you get eaten up by the worms."

What a disturbing answer for me! I couldn't accept it. I knew that life flows on in another life. At the same time, I was plagued by conflicts because I wanted to and should believe my mother. As an adult, she should know. And I, as a child, was not allowed to doubt her testimony.

"If there's something on the other side, I'll give you a sign"

Over the years, I had several conversations with my mother about death as well as philosophical topics. She had no academic background. However, she carried a deep wisdom within and an original way of thinking. Above all, she had a great ability to love, a lot of empathy and respect for nature. In

fact, she was a pantheist. Almost every sentence of hers began with "In nature...", "Nature shows that.... ", "You only have to look at nature..."
Over time, she has slightly changed her attitude towards death. Although she continued to believe in nothing and was convinced that death was "the end" she mentioned that she would contact me if she did encounter something in the afterlife. She would send me a sign.

A decade later, while I was living on a boat in England, my mother paid me a visit. When she arrived, I was very surprised at her overall condition. The mother I had always known as ailing, sad, depressed, pessimistic and tense was suddenly light, cheerful, life-affirming and even physically fit. She was better than ever. We had a wonderful time. She admired nature and was enjoying all and sundry.
Just as in the past, we had philosophical conversations. Especially in the evening when we were both lying in the obscurity of the cabin. Those were special moments for me: the darkness of the night deepened the exchange between us and intensified every feeling. My mother's every word resonated in my ears and every thought form was imprinted in my memory. Since I was very receptive, I was all the more astonished when she suddenly said: "Life definitely goes on. Death is not the end". Her words sounded majestic and carried a real cosmic authority in their expression. My mother was not only convinced, but she spoke from the pure source.
I was so amazed that I fell silent as I simultaneously heard her earlier assumption resonating in my head: "When you're dead, the worms eat you up and it's over".
How could that be?

How could my mother give me a completely opposite answer now?

I knew death wasn't the end. And yet, I had aligned myself with my family's belief system.

And now my dear mother tells me that, of course, life continues after death. And that she will give me a sign.

Shortly after this conversation, she became acutely ill. She was again the weak, sad, sickly woman I had always known. She drove back to France, where she passed away shortly after arriving.

And she gave me a sign.

A few weeks later, my mother appeared to me, looking younger, cheerful, light-hearted, and life-affirming. Exactly as she did during her visit to England. She emanated boundless love and joy. She told me she was fine and free of pain. She looked beautiful and very happy. I could literally feel the bliss she radiated.

Her statement was correct: "It goes on".

The fact that she appeared to me healed many issues between us. It was peace beyond understanding. Karmic entanglements were dissolved. Only love connects us.

PART 2: MY LIFE CRISIS AND MY VOCATION

Meditation and the voice in my head

The life crisis that shattered my worldview at the age of 28 also revealed my purpose in life. Vocation and profession became one. Out of my ability to perceive and read auras, I have made one of my main occupations.

I was guided to excellent teachers like Vicky Wall from Aura Soma. I benefited a great deal from one-on-one instructions from other spiritual teachers, as it is customary in the spiritual tradition. Then I became aware of an inner voice expressing itself both loudly in my head and silently and telepathically. I also received spontaneous knowledge that comes to me like a flash.

Through doubt and hesitation, I tended to unnecessarily obstruct my path with hurdles. I couldn't accept getting the answer or the solution that easily and I created long periods of mental doubt for myself.

I always wanted to check and prove. The rational woman in me who "believed in nothing" - according to my atheistic upbringing - had to question everything. Even if this neurotic tendency made me take many detours, I am grateful for it today. As a result, I have done numerous trainings such as: channeling, mediumship, angel communication, remote viewing, mediumship, animal communication, pendulum, and rod. Therefore, I have developed discernment and a realistic attitude. I have come to the conclusion that no method is 100% accurate. Even more important is the insight that extrasensory perceptions must be coupled with concrete evidence. The information must be factually and emotionally comprehensible. In my international Aura-Medium-Center I expressly insist upon this.

Meditation also confirmed and deepened this knowledge. The meditative state is actually the basis for exploring the subtle realms.

Aura reading – Aura cleansing

Over 3 decades ago, I received the assignment from my guides that I was to conduct annual personal messages. I found it difficult to accept, on the one hand, because I couldn't imagine its practical implementation (How to manage group work and individual channelings at the same time?), on the other hand, because this challenge from spirit was unique for me.
For 3 decades now, between November and March of each year, I have successfully been sharing individual messages for the New Year (current dates on the website: aureliennedauguet.com). I was not given any information how to realize this task. As spirit always respects human´s free will, there was no pressure. However, it seemed the most natural thing to put into practice as I´m aiming at aligning my will with the supreme Will.
My abilities and their development are shown to me from within: I keep getting inspiration or inner impulses that are confirmed by external events. It seems as if the right opportunities are being presented to me on a silver platter. An idea comes to me, then the corresponding situation appears in my real life, which paves the way for me to implement it.
This is how my energetic work called healing hands and the private sessions of aura reading - aura cleaning have become my main tasks. Even if I have never been able to market my work, I have always had enough clients. My inner voice confirms better than any advertising that the flow of my work depends upon my frequency.

Raising my vibration and stabilizing it are exactly the priority I focus on. Thus, it is assuring that my work is authentic.

My inner guidance: my occupation as a lecturer

I have always intentionally initiated new beginnings in my life, as guided by my inner promptings. Once I've mastered something, I rapidly got bored and looked for the next challenge: whether it is a matter of taking on a new role (nurse, therapist, lecturer, book author, shopkeeper) or of moving to another city or even abroad and back.
At some point I needed a career change again. Something that would, as always, spark my enthusiasm. I had attended a weekend course in which the school leader was present as a participant. My resonance to the teaching material was mediocre. I had been successful with aura reading and aura cleansing. However, I was missing something: namely, I was ready to pass on my knowledge. Even if I had plenty of practice teaching in the seminars which I gave in my esoteric shops.
I was going through a difficult phase, as the usual occupation was no longer fulfilling and the new one has not yet been defined. I was just getting back from shopping when my state froze and my attention sharpened: I was hovering over my body and heard the following instruction:
"Call the headmistress, and ask her the following question: do you have someone offering aura therapy as a professional training?"
The voice went on: she will reply in a cheerful voice, "No, not yet. But if you make me a suggestion, we can start in the autumn".

Immediately, I had to struggle with strong doubts. Am I good enough? She will certainly have no interest in aura therapy, etc.!
But the urge to call was so strong that I couldn't resist it.
I called and asked the question as instructed.
The school leader's reply was verbatim and in exactly the same tone as I had heard previously.
I then sat down, completely overwhelmed. The content of the seminar was telepathically dictated to me. It was accepted immediately by the school. And so, I started a successful career in this naturopathy institute.

My inner conflicts: family and spiritual teachers

Although I received countless communications from the higher dimensions, I argued with eternal doubts and succumbed to mood fluctuations. I took the messages apart. I was ashamed and wondered why these things would happen to me? I was torn between the awe-inspiring process and the immediate experience of it. The inputs of my guidance are extremely concrete, physically and emotionally. However, sometimes they show up in a purely spiritual way, when I hear the voice or receive clear images and direct knowledge like a lightning.
I encountered various destructive stages and arguments: "I didn´t deserve it. And maybe the message was not true anyway".
Then came the fear. I was afraid of contacting evil entities. My father and several spiritual teachers who were axed on negativity had warned me about it.
I had a period during which I was visited by the very lively face of Christ in my daily meditation. The frequency that

accompanied these apparitions was very high. "But why should he show up to me if I grew up as an atheist" was my query.

Then, there was the Maria phase associated with various water sources as well as books about the subject and the strange series of synchronicities.

As I attended a remote viewing training, the teacher induced an encounter with angels who wrapped me up in an unearthly love, so that I could channel them effortlessly. I had neither been fond of angel statues or similar items or of the recurring mention of love. But at that moment, with their love pouring through me, I became a clear mouthpiece of these angelic beings.

Again and again, I experienced déjà-vu situations, where I previously had lived this exact scene before in my mind.

Nonetheless, I am well acquainted with the other sides of my personality: In some practical areas of my life, I am rather foolish and clumsy and I do know failure. I used to find it difficult to reconcile these aspects with the deep and wise insights that I received spontaneously.

Moreover, I was concerned about losing touch with reality. Too often, I had known the pitfalls of wishful thinking and illusion, which I also had witnessed in the esoteric scene.

These experiences along with my encounters with the dark entities and with negative egregors have led me to choose authenticity with rigor and clarity.

My special protection

Even though I tended to be scared and uncertain, it is striking how I have frequently taken risks throughout my life. I've always enjoyed traveling alone in Europe, in Russia, in the US and even to Oman - often hitchhiking. I have conducted a lot of adventures such as daring extreme dietary experiments as far as breatharianism as well as various therapies with people I didn´t know, like the floating tank and numerous meditations, therapy groups and other practical testing methods.

I was very curious and naive at the same time. My upbringing, the conversations I shared with my mother and Jean-Jacques Rousseau´s philosophy influenced my outlook on life: man is essentially good.

I was and am still convinced about it. I know that this positive attitude has shaped many of my adventurous situations. I am also aware that I have reliable gut feelings. My confidence is healthy. I am reflected and reasonable. I also have a temper and can fend for myself. I feel lucky.

This is the list my personality (my human aspect) makes when I look back at some dangerous situations wondering how I came out alive and safe.

What does it even mean to be lucky? That was my assumption of the situation at the time. A rather superficial one until I could gain deeper insights.

Years later, while immersed in a trivial activity, I suddenly recalled 2 precise situations from my younger years. In a flash, I floated in an out-of-body state with extensive perception. I was able to perceive not only external events, but also the thoughts, motives and intentions of those around me, as well as my own intentions and actions.

These were some dangerous situations that actually no young woman should face alone.

I was travelling in a car in the mountains, somewhere in Bulgaria together with 4 men. As a matter of fact, I did not know them except for one, the son of the couple I was visiting behind the iron curtain, still under the communist regime. We communicated with a mixture of my bad Russian and with their bad English. At some point, it occurs to me that they are supposed to be at work. I ask them: "How come you got the day off?" They give me a vague answer, telling me not to tell anybody about it. Obviously, something is wrong, but the weather, the mountains and nature are wonderful.

However, as the twilight is slowly coming down, I begin feeling eerie. Unexpectedly, I start "being talked through". To my own surprise, I express myself in a firm and authoritative tone of voice: "Now let's wrap it and let´s go home". The effect of my words is immediate: the men collect their things rapidly and we drive home safely.

Years later, perceiving that setup from a more detached perspective, I then realized that the 4 men definitely were not nurturing the best intentions towards me. Back then, western women had a bad reputation there. I got the insight, that I wasn´t just being lucky. I was actually being protected by my highest instance. My guides showed it to me years later and I express my deepest gratefulness.

I'm lying in a bed in someone´s apartment in Chicago. I am telepathically warned that the situation in the room next door is slowly getting out of hand: people are drinking alcohol and using drugs. I have retired to the bedroom and lie there, fully clothed. The energy is tense and unpredictable. A man´s voice is getting louder. In the dark, I perceive the energies that accompany such gatherings: they feed on fear, violence and confusion. Suddenly, the noisy man bursts into the bedroom and lies on the bed next to me: he is sweating, his face has turned into a grimace, his pupils are dilated and he can only mumble slurred words. His buddies enter the room and watch the scene with frozen expressions. I know that I can by no means count on their help. Suddenly "I am being spoken through" and I say in a clear, deep voice: "It's late now. Let's all go to sleep and we shall see each other tomorrow. Good night." Not only was I surprised by the decisive tone of my voice, but also amazed by its effect on the befuddled guy and his friends: they all wished me good night and immediately left the bedroom.

This is not just having a stroke of luck, as I used to think until I was shown this scene from a higher perspective and from a higher awareness. This is the expression of the highest protection.

Countless similar situations have accumulated in my life. I have come to a point where I accept them with deep gratitude as a token of my spiritual guidance. I am convinced that everybody is similarly protected by a higher power – It makes sense to invoke it and to be forever grateful.

PART 3: REVIEW AND DISCOVERY OF MY SPIRITUAL GUIDES

Contacting my spirit guides

As previously described, my awareness of and connection with my spirit guides was severely impaired.
On the one hand, I felt "never alone", always accompanied. However, I could not clearly and easily accept that I was being guided and protected. I used to constantly question, doubt and even boycott what I saw, felt and heard. I took experiences apart and rationalized them until I came to the conclusion that I had made things up, invented them or even let myself be influenced. However, I always followed the voice in my head. The answers to my questions were so clear that I couldn't ignore them.
In retrospect, it became even more natural to recognize that certain rules and laws apply: Openness is necessary, and the ego should take a back seat and make room for the big presence.
I have also discovered that many practices or widespread information regarding the spirit world are incomplete, undifferentiated, or incorrect. Some of my hesitations or doubts were justified and based on certain experiences. It's as if I had to find out and check the way there through trials and error as well as how to maintain the connection myself. As a result, I took many detours and made it more difficult for myself than necessary. However, it was not a waste of time, as I have been sharpening and training my reasoning mind to minutely examine my intuition. This, in turn, gives me unshakable confidence. As I wrote in my book LIGHT-NUTRITION - MY NEW LIFE AS A BREATHARIAN, I tend to make all the mistakes there is to make. This is how I discover the optimal methods and attitudes that I am then sharing with my students and clients.

That in itself is a huge advantage for my professions as a lecturer and a therapist.

The frequency of the earth and of humanity who is ready to evolve has been greatly increasing in the last decades. Parallel to this elevation of the vibration, the spiritual realms are reaching down, in order to facilitate the contact between the dimensions. Of course, the access is inconsistent and varies from person to person. However, this state of affairs is not new; it has been at work since the great convergence of the 1980s. The characteristics are becoming more visible to a growing number of incarnated souls.

That is why afterlife communication is even more topical and important. It is a matter of contacting not only one's own wisdom and soul knowledge but also entities from higher dimensions, serving as a bridge to cosmic consciousness. That is exactly what is being taught in my aura-medium-center.

Basically, everybody is loved, guided and protected. We all have at least one spirit guide. Other spirits from different levels will join as needed, depending on the life stages we are going through. We are embedded in the cosmos. The distorted energies will do anything to give people the illusion that they are lonely, isolated and disconnected from the bigger picture. In contrast, the all-encompassing security is always there, whether we perceive it or not.

I apologize for trampling, ignoring and misunderstanding the truth of being embedded within the universal forces. I am grateful for the spiritual power and my spirit guides for accompanying, advising, protecting, saving and caring for me over so many years – in spite of my ignorance.

For the time being, I can identify 4 of them specifically.

Joy is the wife of a spiritual teacher of mine. When she was still on earth, she used to send me gifts, selected books and music from the US. She was always friendly and attentive to me. Joy is now my first channeling guide.

Mr. Kistler was my first private teacher and healer in Zurich. He deeply influenced me by passing on his wide knowledge in a down-to-earth manner. He was my psychotherapist from CG Jung school and I took many private lessons over the years. He continues to teach and advises me from beyond.

I already mentioned Dr Barthès, our family doctor in the 1950s and 1960s, in my book "THE CONMAN OR OF LOVING AND DYING". He was against vaccinations and founded the first acupuncture school in France. He contacted me while hovering between life and death. That was a time I was rather stuck in my spiritual evolution and when I was repressing the otherworldly reality. However, he did provide me with tangible confirmation of my perceptions, as he survived and told me firsthand about his near-death experience. As a spirit guide, he is responsible for the healing area. Together with Mr. Kistler, Dr Barthès successfully supported me and inspired me with my discoveries pertaining to my health and balance.

Through her pantheism, my mother has supported me from the spirit world in recent years, particularly with my connection to nature and my practical intuition. She has shown me the power of love, simplicity and emotion and guided and accompanied me on my emotional journeys.

Many other helpers and spiritual teachers are also around me. They constantly provide their help. And if needed, also through the intervention of other beings as required who are mediated by the main spirit guides.

My star siblings unfortunately always feel too distant. However, they are my origins and my real family. An insatiable longing for them drives me forward and torments my heart again and again.

Frank Alper later came forward as a leading spiritual teacher in the unfolding of my mediumship. As a universal channel, he has channeled worldwide for 30 years. In the early 1980's he wrote several books on Atlantis and the therapeutic use of crystals. I met him in Munich and he wanted to teach me channeling, which I then refused because I was afraid of my own abilities and also of being limited by the narrow beliefs of a system. He has inspired me from beyond to found the AURA-MEDIUM-CENTER. He continues to accompany me in his serious, clear and non-intrusive manner. I feel a deep gratitude for him in particular and for all my spirit guides.

"You have all the pieces of the puzzle that she needs"

This is the testimony of a deceased whom I did not know while he was incarnated on earth. He is the husband of a woman I personally met for only 15 minutes. She was part of a fleeting encounter, and at the time I did not get a pleasant impression of her. She then returned abroad, where she lives. Nevertheless, she kept coming to my mind, even though we had only spoken briefly. She was gone now. Why would I keep thinking about her? Especially since I felt no personal connection to her. Somehow, I could not grasp the situation. There was no way I could ignore her. She repeatedly came to my awareness. I took a closer look at her situation in a clairvoyant way.

Spontaneously, I am able to understand why she behaved so awkwardly. She's under a lot of pressure. She is a widow, and she is in charge of an estate that she has been running alone since her husband passed away. She is overwhelmed. She is passive-aggressive and her beliefs and victimhood create a tough life where she sees herself as a lone fighter. Nobody is good enough. Nothing fits. Everyone is cheating on her and being dishonest towards her. While observing her situation, I feel compassion for her. I also realize there is a lesson for me: I shouldn't judge, but rather try and understand the background of her behavior. In fact, I can definitely empathize with her and her reaction. I telepathically ask her for forgiveness. I think, I have now gained the insight contained in this encounter. But she keeps popping up in my mind.

Not only her, but also her husband who is now contacting me from the afterlife planes. I should get in touch with his wife Amelie. I should write to her. She needs help. When I receive such a message, I automatically think that I should do an energetic treatment at distance. What should I offer her? We barely know each other. In no case do I want to say to her: "Your husband instructed from beyond to get in touch with you. What do you exactly need?" No, I will not do that. That's too lurid and who knows whether Amelie is open to the possibility of communicating with the souls who have passed on. I do not know her anyway.

A couple of months go by. And again, she appears in my mind's eye. I sometimes suffer from the helper syndrome. I cannot remain indifferent. Amelie has my business card. I'm sure she will call or write if she needs me in any way.

And so, I had a break from her cropping in my mind. Until her husband turns to me very clearly: "You have all the pieces of the puzzle that she needs". That was a complete mystery! What pieces of the puzzle should I have for someone I barely know and don't particularly like?

"What is it about?" I ask, "What can I do for her?" Then it starts again: I'm supposed to get in touch with her. I'm torn between her husband's directions and my impression of Amelie. I am feeling in a conflict torn in 2 parts: on the one hand, the clear call for help from the hereafter, and on the other hand, I don't feel any real connection to Amelie, even if I can empathize with her situation. Suddenly I think I know what it's all about. Maybe she needs someone to look after the apartment which she owns in the city where I live. Yes, it must be it. If it is helpful, I am ready to look after it for her. I am sincere and would do my best. I'll do that. I text her first. She reports back immediately with a series of worries and problems. Everything is going wrong, she complains. But no, she doesn't need anybody to look after her flat. More challenges are ahead. Things that should be done quickly, urgent situations that have been dragging on for a long time and require immediate solutions. Yes, everything is so bad and there is no one to help her.

Her situation is even more complicated than I realized. There is so much to rectify there. Besides, there is no task that I could assist Amelie with. Or is there?

It suddenly occurs to me that I know someone in the country where she resides who could help her. He even lives an hour away from her. I'm trying to bring together John and Amelie. It doesn't work right away because Amelie, in her stress, entered his phone number incorrectly. There's a back-and-forth situation that she gets unduly upset about. We solve that quickly and easily. She is now enthusiastic about John's support.

I lean back and think: that's it. Wonderful. I am glad I could be of help to Amelie. But it goes further. And indeed, there were a number of circumstances in which I was helpful to her because I had exactly the right information. I knew the right people in her proximity, and I had access to the necessary data.

Amelie´s late husband was right: I had the pieces of the puzzle that she just needed.

This event finally led me to accept and improve my task as a medium.

Here are a few funny examples. They refer to material wishes that I could not fulfill for financial or logistical reasons (I don't have a car). They are specific objects which I desire. But I cannot obtain them for now. For example, I liked these high, wavy mirrors. I would have liked to have one. I had to do without it. Until a few days ago. Right on the street, carefully packed and with the note: "mirror for free". Exactly the kind I wanted! My heart jumps with joy. Immediately, one side of me says: You went so long without. You don't need it anymore. Yes, that's right. But the voice reminds me how much I had wished for such a wavy mirror. The voice tells me: "Take it. Look: it is so well wrapped up for you. Carry it under your arm. It will make you happy. You asked for it and now it's here for". So, I received it 1 year later, for free and 300 meters from home. Thank you so much!

Afterlife communication with the deceased

Now I would like to give some examples of the experiences I have had over the years.

An important factor is that I treat the deceased with respect: I invite them and leave it open to who wants to appear. This means that nobody is forced to appear, but rather the souls who are most helpful to the client in the here and now come forward. From the higher levels, the priorities are different and, above all, easier to set than from our earthly point of view. The souls in the afterlife have a higher perspective on the entire situation and its connections.

We must not lose sight of how "short-sighted" we are and how controlled we are by conditioning, prejudice, fear and our ego.

Dealing and working with the spiritual dimensions requires not only trust, but the ability to actively implement this trust. This includes an infinite assurance of doing the right thing in the moment, with no concrete "human evidence" or "guarantees" or actual confirmation. This requires a certain willingness to let go, and inner freedom, regardless of the outcome. The required unconditional presence and surrender to spiritual guidance in the present moment is the basis. The individual steps, one after the other, can be visualized as a picture. Overcoming a chasm with a rope, like walking a tightrope. Highly concentrated in the present, step by step, without even looking ahead. The ego doesn't like that at all.

In the afterlife communication we make ourselves receptive to the messages that come from a higher vantage point. They may sound surprising because they transcend our warranties. "I wouldn't have thought of it myself" "I hadn't considered it that way" we will often say.

As much as we are willing to accept an expanded perspective, we are receptive to a quality of information that transcends our wishful thinking, our hopes, and our narrow view. The information is therefore ego-free, individually valid, adapted to the person and their current circumstances and generally ethical, because they are not self-serving, but are in harmony with the highest good.

Example

A client I know well, Jasmin, wanted to establish contact with a distant aunt. She had some questions for her because this family member has been left out of the clan and kept away from the inheritance and she was practically never mentioned. I explain to Jasmin that she is welcome to keep her aunt as a target. However, I will invite those souls who have an essential message for my client to come forward.

The first person I see is a child. The period corresponds to the period between the two world wars. The boy is playing near a pond. First, my client has no relation to this boy. She was expecting an aunt or maybe a female child, but definitely not a boy. She cannot make anything out of my description. There is a small wall. In the background I see a dog barking behind a fence. He has plenty of space but prefers to walk along the fence and greet people. The scene looks idyllic. But the atmosphere is getting more and more tense. A feeling of tightness in my chest takes my breath away. I'm the little boy and I can't breathe anymore.

"The dog, the boy... no, I have no idea who that is. We had a dog but not in a meadow behind the fence. No, unfortunately...." I hear Jasmin on the phone.

I continue to describe what I perceive.

Suddenly, a gush of emotion comes out of Jasmin.

"Oh, I know! My grandfather rushed to the rescue of this little boy when he was drowning in the pond! Now I know. Yes, I know who he is. I don't know his name, but I've often heard from him and how my grandfather wanted to save him and gave him first aid. Unfortunately, in vain, because he died in the hospital. Yeah, that was a big thing back then with that neighbor kid. My grandfather was considered a hero because he selflessly jumped into the water for the child. I was told this story several times as a child. I'm 60 years old now, that was a long time ago." continues Jasmin.

I receive one more piece of important information from the boy. His soul is infinitely grateful, and he feels so connected to the family his grandfather comes from that he continues to bless them. In particular, he protects Roberto, Jasmin's only son. Yes, the boy from back then is there for Roberto and is happy to take him under his wing.

Jasmin was amazed and whispered:

"He probably has no idea about that..."

Thus, this frame or the constellation dissolves together with the impressions that belong to it.

Now a completely different picture emerges: a young woman behind a counter. Her hairstyle gives me a clue about the time before the outbreak of WW2. She makes a light-footed impression on me. She is in a good mood, almost careless. She stands there and moves happily. She talks about simple, everyday things and her positive mood is contagious. I receive no further notices. Jasmin doesn't feel any resonance with her. It's about a person she didn't know.

These are Jasmin's words to the 2nd person who has now appeared.

However, I am gifted with further impressions from the afterlife and describe them truthfully. The young woman's frivolity and her unshakable good humor are at the forefront. She is around 30. Everyone is drawn to her lightness. Jasmin is still silent. But I can feel her searching her mind for memories.

"Yes, I mean... That's the mother. I know exactly who that is. She got pregnant by a distant nephew. This young woman had a bad reputation. It was said that she had tempted him. The nephew from our wealthy family was 16 years old at the time."

Then Jasmin continues:

"This young woman is THE AUNT'S MOTHER! As an illegitimate child, she was raised by her grandparents because she couldn't stay with her mother."

Now the young woman wants to tell her the following: "It wasn't that bad. My daughter (who grew up with her grandparents) liked it. She got everything she needed for her life. She lacked for nothing." This statement sounds a bit extraordinary, because illegitimate mothers and children were severely "discriminated against", as one would say today.

Now Jasmin is very quiet again. I can feel her head working intensely. After a few minutes she begins uncertainly:

"I originally wanted to get in touch with the aunt, the daughter of the light-footed person, to offer her compensation for what she experienced as an illegitimate child."

"But the young woman confirms that her daughter got everything she needed," I repeat as a mouthpiece for the soul that appeared as the aunt's mother.

"That's nice to know," replies Jasmin. "I just wanted to clear all the karma. But if all is well…. Then it's time to let go."

Jasmin was very surprised when she met her aunt's mother. She is grateful not only for making contact, but for the pacification that came from it. She is grateful for the peace she finds through the news and for the karmic bond release.

A few days later I receive the following email from Jasmin:

"I have the following additional information about my encounters with the little boy:

I hesitated to tell my son Roberto (also that this little boy is there for him). Roberto doesn't know his name, only the rough outline of the story. So, I left the picture of my deceased grandfather, which I "accidentally" found 3 weeks ago in my dad's estate, on the table. Roberto jumped at it immediately. Well, I told him about our phone call - namely about the afterlife communication.

Roberto said: "You know mom, lately I've often thought about the fact that my grandpa wanted to save someone's life. And a few days ago (this coincides with our telephone appointment), I thought very intensely about the little boy.

Isn't that touching? And it confirms you / us so much.
Thank you for this gift."
Written by Jasmin on January 31, 2022.

I, too, feel a deep respect for the synchronistic connections, the details and their coherence that I could never have imagined. It is not just about the encounter with a certain deceased, but also about the message, the advice and the new insights that are transmitted by the people on the other side. They are actually present, and they care deeply about supporting us from their higher vantage point. The deceased who accompany us are souls who have committed themselves to service to others as opposed to energy centered on their own selves, distorting divine order and ultimately seeking power drain rather than power gain.

Now I would like to offer short examples with different positive effects of afterlife communication.
Legal examples of people who left injustice or acknowledged their mistakes and asked for forgiveness, like the young man who was blinded by the Hitler Youth. Only later, from the other perspective, did he realize that he was walking a path that actually contradicted his fundamental values. Some have been punished on Earth and realized that they have made the wrong "choice". His escape brought him a peaceful life far abroad, beyond the veil he was reminded of the act that cosmic laws were not honored.
Then we meet souls who have not been sincere and have stolen, embezzled goods or funds. Under this category we also find those who have stolen an inheritance. A client was given a ritual by a deceased cousin to break the family curse. I will

always remember how the client said with great gratitude: "You helped me a lot. Not just me, but my entire family."

Some "secrets" are clarified through afterlife communication, so that its contents are shared with family members, especially older ones. The connections that are overlooked or "forgotten souls" are recognized spontaneously by parents or grandparents. Synchronicities play a special role: e.g. A gift from Bertha which was mentioned in the message from beyond the veil but could not be identified during the session. Only in hindsight was the physical and psychological description of Bertha recognized by her mother's memories. Her gift at the time, the necklace with the 3 hearts, was just found in a box when my client, Anna, moved to Bertha's former property a few decades later.

Anna wrote in the report that followed the communication beyond the veil:

"Very fascinating! I will definitely allow the information to sink into my consciousness and continue to reveal the truth beyond death. I can only sincerely thank you and the respective visitors from the afterlife".

Automatic writing and other ways of communication (animals, painting, environment exploration)

I've always loved writing: essays, school reports, letters, journals, philosophy exams, etc. I started auto-writing early in my life without knowing what it meant. I've always liked to perform a ritual before starting it. I needed order around me. My desk needed to be clean and tidy. When I wrote the first sentence, it sometimes took me a few tries before I actually found myself in the flow. The writing had to be right, ideas in my head or a specific project were a prerequisite and I had to feel a certain energy right from the start. If it wasn't right, I had to start all over again. Over time I realized that I would write down the text that I heard in my head. I used this talent more and more for the writing of my books. I have later observed myself receiving recommendations and descriptions of my clients' inner workings as I tune into them spiritually. I use this ability as individual counselling in my PERSONAL CHANNELINGS (see my website: aureliennedauguet.com). Many people have gained great, concrete help from it. The advantage is that you can read the text over and over again. With each reading one discovers a deeper meaning and messages that were not initially apparent. Of course, the client must be independent in their thinking and able to adapt the text to their own personal circumstances.

I would now like to go into detail about the term "automatic writing". Strictly speaking, she knows that the medium's hand is guided "from outside" until words and sentences emerge while she is in a trance. My method is different and consists in being aware and very present because I hear the words in my head, and I have to keep up with them or I lose the flow. So, I am highly concentrated and I receive guidance from my higher guidance as well as images or feelings and sensual impressions such as taste, colors, narrowness, breadth to name a few. One could also speculate that it is some kind of telepathy. However, I cannot force the flow: I do feel that it is there, and sometimes in a very urgent way. I am infinitely grateful for that.

The school program also includes communication with animals. They are living beings with a soul. They carry the awareness of universal consciousness. Basically, the whole nature has a soul and is very individual. Capturing individuality requires developed empathy and great adaptability. This is about the multifaceted expression of unity that is only accessible through respect and humility.

I have a short example: I wanted to get in touch with an older, wise cat. Since he was rather reserved, I tried to draw his attention to me. In vain. Finally, he gave me a rather unfriendly look and said briskly that he already knew me and that he was appalled by my question.

"Oh dear, that's a bad start for soul-to-soul communication." I mumbled to myself. Also, I was amazed at what he told me.

"How do you know me? How do you know my question?"

"You prepared yourself thoroughly for the questioning. I heard the whole thing."

"Officially now, I asked why cats are so lazy and need so much sleep, up to 16 hours a day?"

"Only humans are constantly active and so intensely directed outwards. We are adaptable and highly focused in what we do. Hunting can be exhausting. But the real reason for our long sleep lies in our ability to travel to other dimensions and recharge our batteries there. We cats belong to the world soul and make our contribution through our collective soul wisdom. We are dimension blasters. We connect the worlds. We connect with other souls from our cat collective. We are not lazy, but we work in the beyond for the balance of all living things. We live here and there. People should be inspired by us and turn more inwards".

He disappeared from view as soon as he delivered his answer. I hope he understood my thanks and apologies for the disturbance. I would have liked to ask more questions, but I am grateful for this detailed answer and the pictures he sent me. He actually seemed to be on other levels and to have an important task.

I can't paint, I can't draw, I've never learned it and I'm not gifted for it either. I was directed to draw a couple of times, however. One such example is the drawing on the front cover of my book, LIGHT-NUTRITION - MY NEW LIFE AS A BREATHARIAN. It was created at 4:00 am and shows one of the souls that accompanied me during the light nurturing process. The automatic aspect of painting is encouraged in the channeling training, for the inspiration within the framework of artistic expression is the supreme influence of the spirit in the form of the muse.

The exploration of the environment is also part of the training and is expressed by enabling the medium to describe, feel and see the environment of the subject. Such perceptions can happen spontaneously. However, they require thorough mastery on the part of the recipient.

PART 4: HIGHER COMMUNICATION

Introduction to the ethical foundations of the aura-medium-center.

A respectful treatment of all beings forms the basis of our work.

FREE WILL: the client's free will and privacy must be respected. It's not about spying or getting intimate details. Abuse of mediumistic and other abilities can lead to loss of talent and karmic balance. Respecting the deceased or other otherworldly entities (Ascended Masters, known personalities, angels, spirit guides, etc.) is the basis of valuable higher communication. Lying or forced messages represent fraud and transgression. Such discrepancies are registered by the higher self.

The SELF-RESPONSIBILITY of the medium, as well as that of the client, is essential. The deceased and the spirit guides are eager to help and provide information. However, they always give you the opportunity to decide for yourself. And that is exactly what the medium should respect towards the client. The opportunity to make a choice voluntarily represents not only a special chance to exercise free will, but an incomparable situation for advancing on the spiritual path and achieving karmic balance. This fact is related to personal priorities, ideals, creed and service to the greater good. Afterlife communication is a service for the common good, not self-expression.

The most important requirement is: DO NO DAMAGE. The medium takes responsibility for the message. The client takes responsibility for his interpretation of the message.

The OWN FREQUENCY is decisive for which energies we attract as a medium: that means permanent work on oneself.

Everything is communication and we are all channeling

The cells communicate with each other, the planets with each other, the animals, the trees, etc. Everything is connected and in constant exchange. Interdependence reigns throughout creation. The well-known saying about the butterfly wing, which influences events on the other side of the world, symbolizes the interconnectedness of all existence. It comes from mysticism, metaphysics and quantum philosophy.
Since we are part of the big picture and at the same time RECEIVER AND TRANSMITTER of frequencies, we have to be aware of what we want to absorb, convert and forward.
In fact, we all channel non-stop. By that, I mean the energy that we pass on to the universe, both consciously and unconsciously: the bad mood, the compliments, the joy, the impatience, the wrong information, the prayer, the positive intention, the envious looks, etc. In a nutshell: everything we give of ourselves.
So, knowing this, when we decide to pass on HIGHER INFORMATION, it makes sense to look at what our basic intent is.
All this represents our CONTRIBUTION to the world´s soul.
In this special training, we want to establish a connection between the higher COMMUNICATION OF THE HEART (Ananda Khanda) and the higher INSPIRATION OF THE SPIRIT (6th chakra). This corresponds to the colors of our website (royal blue and turquoise). This is Aquarian Age communication.

The Alchemy of Channeling and Transdimensionality

It is about traveling between the worlds and connecting them in a conducive and clear way to express their information. For this, we maintain the CLARITY of our channel.

The dimensions we contact are a MIRROR of our intention and attitude.

For this, the studying medium has to deal with his ELEMENTAL LEVEL (aura and chakras). His ability to master FEELING-THINKING is the secret to his success. This means a profound self-discovery at the same time.

Every person has special dispositions. Personal gifts are taken into account in this curriculum and supported individually through individual sessions and through the appropriate choice of the different mediumship and channeling methods (see Your New Skills below)

We are not only multidimensional but also transdimensional beings.

Real commitment and consistency are prerequisites.

Clear evidence: the inner logic of spiritual practice

Spiritual clarity is based on authenticity and coherence. In other words, the intuitive work has to have real substance: it has to be empirical, make sense and be helpful. The higher communication is a service to human beings and their progression on their spiritual path. It is anchored in reality.

The interpretation and handling of the transmitted material from the medium are thoroughly analyzed.

Regardless of how simple or complex the message may be, it should bring an increase in vitality, joie de vivre and quality of life in other beings (humans, animals, plants, buildings, projects, etc.).

Sense and purpose of the training courses and their content

In this training, you will learn to EARTH, PROTECT, and CLEAR your energies.
You will learn to increase your SELF-PERCEPTION and AWARENESS of your environment.
You will achieve a deep SERENITY through the UNION of your will with the higher will of your spiritual instance or authority.
You will discover your versatility and at the same time your individuality and its special dispositions. You will develop this in module 2: there you have the opportunity to SPECIALIZE thoroughly in at least 2 methods.
Your general spiritual DEVELOPMENT is ACCELERATED by your INCREASE OF VIBRATION.
You are able to receive higher knowledge as well as down-to-earth, meaningful messages.

You develop both: your THEORETICAL KNOWLEDGE and your PRACTICAL TALENTS. These can be used professionally, privately, therapeutically, psychotherapeutically and spiritually, independently once you have completed the entire training.

You will receive a seminar participation confirmation with details of the modules and the exact number of hours. The number of theory and practical training hours, as well as the individual coaching hours and individual sessions, are also entered on the certificate.

Theoretical and practical trainings of the AURA-MEDIUM-CENTER:

42

1. CHANNELING MEDIUM TRAINING: OVERVIEW OF THE CURRICULUM

2. AURA THERAPY TRAINING: OVERVIEW OF A 6 W/E CURRICULUM

CHANNELING MEDIUM TRAINING: OVERVIEW OF THE CURRICULUM

MODULE 1

Preparation and first steps of higher communication
Awareness of one's own subtle energy:
- Aura and chakras
- Focusing the attention
- Internalizing the focus
- Protection, grounding, central channel opening
- Increasing own frequency
- Encountering and interacting with the Higher Self
- Inklings, inspiration, and intuition
- Quality, meaning and truthfulness
- Personal shortcomings and talents
- Sense and formulate
- Awareness of the environment
- The channeling medium´s logbook

- Individual Sessions: 1 Hour Aura Reading – Aura Cleansing and Recommendations

- Personal coaching: Individual questions and technical topics / opportunities for improvement.
- Practice sessions

MODULE 2

- Cleaning and clearing of the field and rooms
- Feel the flow of energy in yourself and see it in others

- Contacting spirit guides
- Receiving messages
- validity of the information
- Dealing with channeled information: neutrality, interpretation, responsibility
- The causes of errors
- The role of ego, imagination and confabulation

MODULE 3

In Module 3, a brief overview of the various contacts is explained. Two of those special mediumistic techniques are chosen and thoroughly learned
Methods and tools as well as specialization to choose from
- Making contacts and communicating 2during your sleep
- Automatic writing, written communication
- Contact with nature, communication with animals
- Boost higher communication with dowsing
- Drawing, painting, sketching
- The 5 senses + 1 sense, feelings and emotions
- Distance perception and remote viewing
- Contact with the deceased
- Angelic Communication and Ascended Masters
- Body readings
- Galerie Readings
- Person-related reading (psychic readings)
- Contact with historical people
- Spaces and Fields Readings

- Personal coaching on individual interests and personal talents

MODULE 4

Learning and practicing the 2 specializations which have been chosen the previous weekend.
- Individual session
- Personal coaching
- Practice session

MODULE 5

The Sacred Triangle of Ethics and Interaction:
- With Clients and with Spirit Guides
- Intensification of contact through rock crystals
- Preparation and cleaning of rooms
- Working as a medium
- Working as a media consultant
- Being a clear, healthy medium: Fear-free, physical activity, and general mental hygiene
- Questions and answers: The medium as a mouthpiece
- Death: the great adventure
- Travel between dimensions

- Aura reading

- Individual coaching
- Practice session

MODULE 6

- The pineal gland
- The Ananda Khanda
- The meditative state
- The direct path
- Symbols and their own symbolic language
- Clairvoyance
- The feeling-thinking of the new time
- The individual contribution to the big picture
- Protocol for a comprehensive reading
- Independence and care of the client

- Individual session
- Personal coaching
- Practice session

AURA THERAPY TRAINING: OVERVIEW OF A 6 W/E CURRICULUM

Aura therapy supports and completes each therapeutic measure, as it includes the subtle aspects of man. Health first originates in the auric dimension.
This aura therapy training enables the AURA COUNCELLOR to clear and harmonize the aura and thus to accompany and strengthen the client in his development and regeneration. The aura counsellor is able to independently ascertain various aura pathologies and to balance them with energetic methods particularly adapted to aura work. The wide knowledge as well as the deepening of the perception both constitute an enrichment and an expansion of consciousness for the day-to-day life and for the professional career.

The imparted knowledge is grounded, as it is anchored in both theory and practice. Aura surgery is also part of this exceptional training. We are awakening our latent spiritual perceptions in a pragmatic manner. The conscious therapist of the new era is thus born.

SEMINAR CONTENTS

MODULE 1

1.1   The global aura
1.2   Aura awareness
1.3   Aura sensitivity
1.4   Traditional knowledge of the aura: famous researchers
1.5   demystification

MODULE 2

MODULE 3

MODULE 4

MODULE 5

5.1   methods of protection including self-protection
5.2   Thorough Aura cleansing
5.3   Complete treatment with semi-precious stones (lithotherapy): a spiritual experience
5.4   Amputation: aura work as support of the medical treatment
5.5   Prophylactic work in the aura: aura work as anti-aging
5.6   Previous incarnations
5.7   The astral body and the astral aura
5.8   The mental body and the mental aura
5.9   Aura perception in person and as remote perception
5.10   One report case
5.11   One practice hour
5.12   feedback round
5. 13   Questions and answer

MODULE 6

6.1   Aura surgery
6.2   Extirpations
6.3   Unwished for energies and entities: Parasites in the aura
6.4   Aura harmonizing as completing method to other methods and treatments
6.5   Aura care by psychological issues
6.6   Aura work for plants and animals
6.7   The aura protocol
6.8   Ethical connections: Organ donation and karma
6.9   Discovering the inner angel
6.10   Feedback round

6.11   One hour practice
6.12   Questions and answers
6.13   presentation of the certificate for the complete
        training as aura counsellor

Changes and improvements making the teaching mode more
individual and adapted to the student´s requirements will be
regularly uploaded on the website:
aura-medium-zentrum.com

Dear reader!
It is important to me to be passing on my knowledge to you.
This is basic knowledge of the new era. The raising of the
earth frequency represents a huge opportunity for the
unfolding of our forgotten and repressed abilities within.
Our awakening potential lends us the opportunity to uncover
the illusion and the lies. Thus, we rediscover our true dignity
as humans.

General contact: aureliennedauguet.com

Special contact for mediumship sessions and training as well
as for aura reading sessions and aura therapy training:
                    aura-medium-center.com

Bibliography

Aurélienne Dauguet

Guide to your cosmic energies

Aura discovery

Only published in German language.

ISBN 978-3-944700-02-1 (Paperback)

ISBN 978-3-944700-12-0 (e-book)

Everything that is alive possesses an aura.
To perceive energies and subtle
emanations is part of the natural talents of living beings.
Rediscovering this opens up a fresh, new look at everyday life
and broadens horizons.
The book "Travel Guide to your Cosmic Energies - Aura
Discovery" takes the reader on a journey of discovery into the
various levels and dimensions of the human aura.
It contains both theoretical treatises on the different layers of
the aura, such as the etheric body, the emotional body or the
mental body, as well as practical exercises for the correct
handling of the aura.

Only available in German.

Aurélienne Dauguet

AURATHERAPY

for DOCTORS, THERAPISTS

and interested laymen

Only published in German language.

ISBN 978-3-944700-42-7 (Paperback)

ISBN 978-3-944700-72-4 (e-book)

This book consists of two parts:

In this textbook, the focus is on the theoretical background, on the aura and its different subtle layers. Energetic approaches to the subtle anatomy are considered. The various aura pathologies and their straightening are treated in detail. The clairvoyant access to the past and future, to incarnational experiences, to prophylactic aura care and to aura surgery are presented and integrated into the therapeutic framework.

This useful book contains practice-oriented exercises that train the therapist's subtle perceptions, and techniques that maintain, protect, clarify, harmonize and treat the aura and its subtle dimensions. It also contains testimonials that support the theory and implementation of aura therapy, as well as inventions by the author.

Only available in German.

Aurélienne Dauguet

AURATHERAPIE

für
ÄRZTE,
THERAPEUTEN
und
interessierte
LAIEN

LEHRBUCH
und
PRAXISBUCH

MERANO-VERLAG

Aurélienne Dauguet

LIGHT-NUTRITION

MY NEW LIFE AS A BREATHARIAN

Published in English, French and German language.

ISBN: 978-3-944700-18-2 (paperback)

ISBN: 978-3-944700-28-1 (e-book)

This is the author's account of her light nourishment process. She describes how she managed to switch from "normal" food to photon nourishment. This report underlines the transformations during the first year of her new life with light nourishment.

This description is authentic, down to earth, clear and simple.

The purpose of her contribution is to facilitate the understanding and spiritual access to light nourishment in a human and realistic way.

In no way is this book an encouragement to practice breatharianism. This process is a purely internal one and can only be a call from the soul. There is nothing to prove and no one to convince.

For the author, the choice to convert into the Prana mode was one of the deepest most relevant in her life, along with the freedom to stop or continue the light nourishment at any time.

French edition:

NOURRITURE LUMINEUSE

MA NOUVELLE VIE AVEC LE PRANISME

ISBN: 978-3-944700-07-6 (paperback)

ISBN: 978-3-944700-67-0 (e-book)

German edition:

Mein neues Leben mit der Lichtnahrung

ISBN 978-3-944700-55-7 (paperback)

ISBN 978-3-944700-75-5 (e-book)

Aurélienne Dauguet

CREATING A NEW SELF-IMAGE

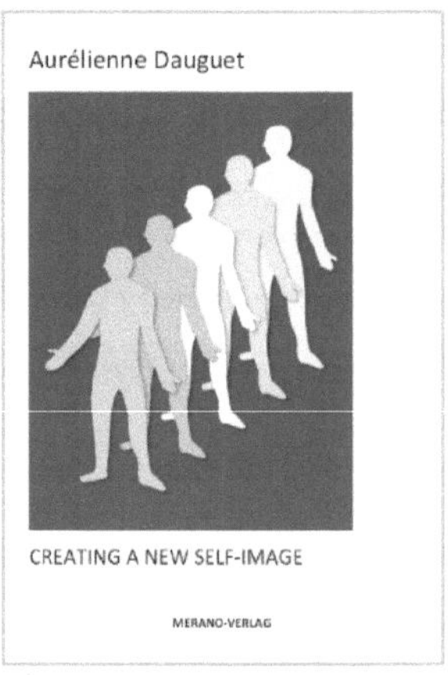

ISBN: 978-3-944700-24-3 (Paperback)

ISBN: 978-3-944700-34-2 (e-book)

Am I just the way I am and always have been and there is nothing to be changed about? Am I also there on earth to discover, explore, develop and express myself and my being? Or am I incarnated here to refine and ennoble my personality and to connect it in alignment with my essence?

I progress into the world, self-determined and authentic, remembering my inherent divine spark. As a creator and in harmony with my higher self, I express my eternal and multidimensional aspects in everyday life.

This encouraging manual about self-knowledge throws a transformative light on the humans as spiritual beings embedded within the current phase of upheaval and breakthrough. The metamorphosis is in full swing. The necessity and the responsibility to create an upgrade of our humanness lies in the hands of each individual. A new personal self-image directly creates and contributes to a differentiated identity of the entire humanity.

Aurélienne Dauguet

The Conman

or

Of loving and dying

ISBN: 978-3-944700-29-8 (paperback)

ISBN: 978-3-944700-89-2 (e-book)

This true story gives amazing insights into karmic contexts and old beliefs that display outdated behavior.

Unexpected connections prevail and are revealed during this exceptional journey to Normandy in the purpose of meeting with a respected author.

Similar to the unfolding of the images of a kaleidoscope, different fates unfold from ancient Egypt to a liberating future full of luminous promises. Rich in insights which confront unacceptable traditional and relationships patterns, the spotlight of consciousness shines on them, in order to transform and heal them.

Reflections and mental abilities underpin every day of the stay in northern France. Eternally valid principles stand out from the entertaining story and lend us a deeper understanding of one's own life, including the processes of loving and dying.

Aurélienne Dauguet

Healthy boundaries

ISBN 978-3-944700-22-9
(paperback)

ISBN 978-3-944700-92-2
(e-book)

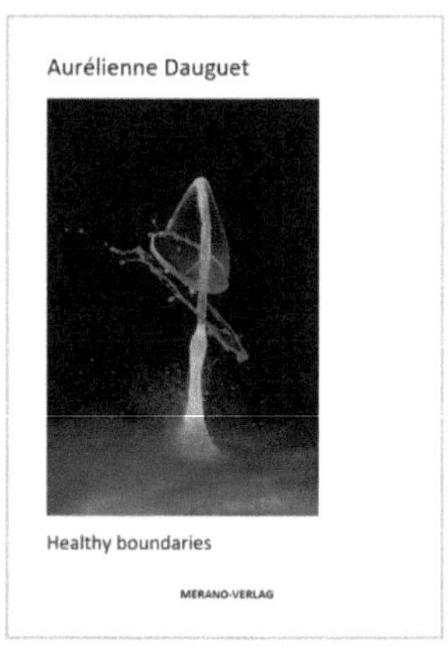

Consideration, goodwill and respect for the space and the free will of our fellow humans is part and parcel of the interaction between people of the new aera.

Not only between persons but also within our own unity as individual, do we practice mindfulness towards our body, our emotional aspect, our cognitive abilities as well as towards the spiritual dimensions of our very being.

In her 12th book (comprising the complete publications in German, French and English), Aurélienne Dauguet deals with the profound topic of building up healthy boundaries on all levels of our individual beingness and also within the collective realms of life.

Politeness, goodwill, and a humanist approach are indispensable, also in contact with people, with whom our opinions differ.

Ethical consequences are attached to our relationships whether we act with respect of their freedom and their free-will or not. It is a duty to encounter conscious life with appreciation. On the other hand, the infringement upon the development of other human beings definitely represents one of the heaviest karmic burden possible.

About the author

Aurélienne Dauguet (born 1953 in Paris) has had a pronounced subtle perception ability since her youth. Initially working as a nurse (also as a registered RMN), today she now teaches as a lecturer at the well-known naturopathy schools in Germany and Switzerland for aura therapy, subtle radionics, the dying process perceived from a holistic point of view, spiritual healing, etc.

The current teaching offers are available from the Paracelsus schools.

Further training: lithotherapy, aura work, aromatherapy, flower and gemstone essences, radiesthesia, subtle radionics (without device), "Radionic Practitioner" according to the "British Radionic Association" and with David Tansley, Aura Soma training with Vicky Wall. Aurélienne Dauguet was one of the very first Aura Soma teachers.

Teaching and seminars on the subject of the aura take place across Europe.

For the last 35 years, she has been practicing Aura reading and Aura cleansing, automatic writing as individual sessions, individual teaching and distant support together with radionics in German, English and French per zoom or by telephone.

If you are interested, please see contact details.

Contact:
Aurélienne Dauguet
Schießgrabenstrasse 28
86150 Augsburg
Tel: 0049 821/45 40 77 44

WEBSITES: aureliennedauguet.com
             aura-medium-zentrum.com